Baton Twirling Master

Baton Twirler - Step by Step Moves & Instructions

By Susan Style

Copyright and Trademarks

Disclaimer and Legal Notice

Receive Free Baton Twirling Videos

You can also join our FREE newsletter and receive baton twirling videos. These detail lots of amazing moves and tricks you can perform, just like the pros! - Details at the back of this book.

Table of Contents

Table of Contents

Table of Contents

Table of Contents

Chapter 1 – Introduction to Baton Twirling

Baton twirling is an activity that combines dance and gymnastic moves for the coordinated manipulation of single or multiple metal rods or batons. Twirlers work to create visual images with their moves through intricate patterns that require precision, timing, and dexterity.

The sport requires excellent physical coordination and fine motor control as well as flexibility, physical fitness, and an aesthetic sense. Although often associated with the sport of football in the American South, twirling has its origins in Asia and Western Europe.

In various applications, including military displays, the items twirled might include rifles, or "maces," which are larger batons, more like a staff, and now often used by marching band drum majors.

Interest in baton twirling is world wide, with three governing bodies for the sport:

- World Baton Twirling Federation (WBTF)
- World Twirling Association (WTA)
- The Global Alliance of National Baton Twirling & Majorette Associations (NBTA)

The WBTF and the NBTA host a world championship competition, while the WTA hosts a number of events in which the other entities do not participate.

The membership of the WBTF includes:

- Australia
- Belgium
- Brazil
- Canada
- Catalonia
- Croatia
- England
- France
- Germany
- Hungary
- Ireland
- Italy
- Japan
- Netherlands
- Norway
- Scotland
- Seychelles
- Slovenia
- South Africa
- Sweden
- Switzerland
- United States

The members of the NBTA include:

- Belgium
- Bulgaria
- Canada
- Croatia
- Czech Republic
- England
- France

- Germany
- The Netherlands
- Ireland
- Italy
- Norway
- Romania
- Russia
- Scotland
- Slovenia
- Spain
- Switzerland
- Ukraine
- United States

As a competitive event, baton twirling has continued to develop in both appeal and complexity. A simple search of YouTube for the phrase "baton twirling" returns almost 50,000 clips including routines from the World Championships.

If you spend time viewing these clips, you'll see that styles vary greatly by region, and many advanced routines include elements that can only be described as interpretive dance.

Learning twirling is very much a mentoring activity. Skills are best passed from one knowledgeable twirler to a novice with hands on correction of fundamentals like body posture, hand and arm positioning, and timing.

While you can certainly make progress working with online video sources and the instructions and illustrations in this book, to truly become skilled in the sport, you should find someone to work with you one on one.

As you begin learning the fundamentals and advanced moves outlined here, remember:

- Make sure you have learned each twirl correctly before you move on to the next.
- Perform each twirl slowly in the beginning, concentrating on the smoothness of the moves and transitions.
- Always concentrate on maintaining correct posture.
- Keep your feet close together and well aligned.
- Keep the hand not in use either on your waist or hip with the fingers held closely together.
- Smile naturally and give the appearance of enjoying the activity.

Do not worry about cultivating speed in your routines in the beginning. It's more important to master the moves and to be able to smoothly combine them before you develop the aggressive style you'll see displayed by world champions.

Illustration of a Baton

Measuring Correct Baton Length

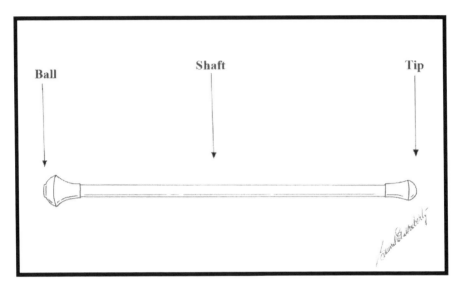

1. Stand erect and extend one arm straight ahead parallel to the floor.

2. Have a friend use a tape measure or yard stick to measure from the base of your neck just above your shoulder to the top of your middle finger.

3. If your measurement falls in between the available baton sizes, go one side up.

Based on ages, the following are approximate appropriate lengths:

Age 1-4 - 18 inches / 45 cm
Age 5-7 - 20 inches / 51 cm

Age 8-10 - 22 inches / 56 cm
Age 11-12 - 24 inches / 61 cm
Age 13-14 - 26 inches / 66 cm
Age 15+ - 28 inches / 71 cm

If an individual is tall or unusually small for their age, increase or decrease the measurement by 1-2 inches / 2.54-5.08 cm.

Holding the Baton

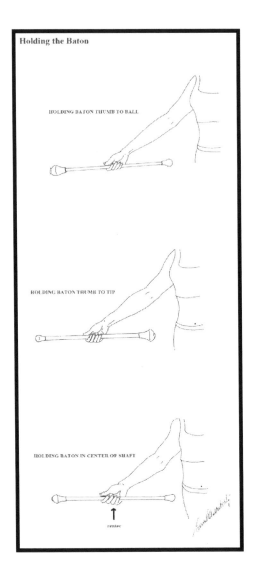

Hold the baton as shown in the adjacent illustration. In most cases your thumb will be toward the ball unless otherwise indicated in the instructions for the specific twirl.

How to March

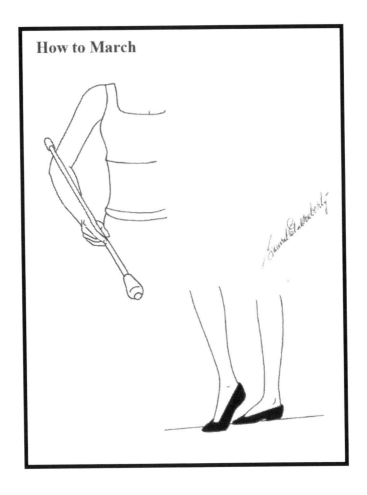

How to March

1. Your posture when marching should be straight and tall with your shoulders held back and your head high.

2. Hold your baton as if it were a pen or pencil in a position to begin writing, with the ball pointed toward the ground.

3. Take the first step with your left foot, toes pointed toward the ground. Touch the ground first with the ball of your foot. Make sure to raise your knees high in an exaggerated, but crisp step.

4. Allow your left hand to swing naturally with your fingers held together. As you practice walking in this way, the motion of your baton will become more natural as well.

Chapter 2 – Twirling Fundamentals

Horizontal Twirl – Right Hand

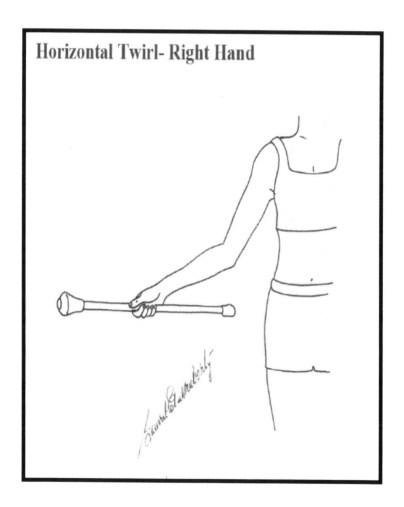

Horizontal Twirl - Right Hand

1. Hold your baton in the center of the staff with your thumb toward the ball. Extend your right arm.

2. Move the ball over the top of your arm in a horizontal motion. Think of the baton as a plate you're balancing to keep the food from sliding off.

3. The tip of the baton is under your arm at the bottom.

The motion is all in your wrist. Concentrate on keeping the shaft of the baton level.

Horizontal Twirl – Left Hand

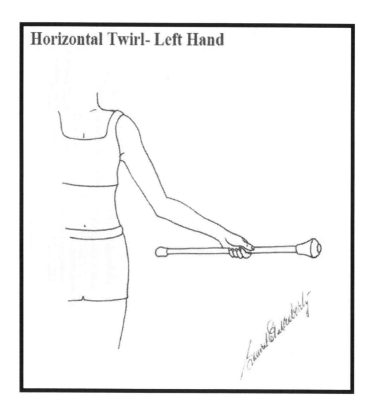

Horizontal Twirl – Left Hand

1. Hold your baton in the center of the staff with your thumb toward the ball. Extend your left arm.

2. Move the ball over the top of your arm in the same horizontal motion you used with your right hand.

3. Remember that the tip of the baton is under your arm at the bottom.

The motion is all in your wrist. Concentrate on keeping the shaft of the baton level.

Horizontal Twirl – Pass From Right Hand to Left

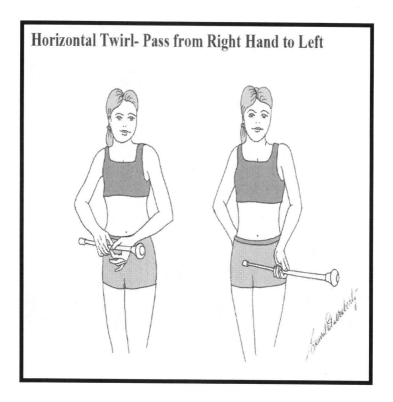

Horizontal Twirl- Pass from Right Hand to Left

Horizontal Twirl – Pass From Right Hand to Left

1. With the right hand, perform a horizontal twirl. Slowly put your left hand on the baton, forming an "O" with the thumb and index finger.

2. Take the baton into the left hand, continuing the motion to the right.

3. The twirl should be in the same direction as the baton passes from your right hand and into your left.

4. Maintain a horizontal plane with the baton throughout the twirl.

Horizontal Twirl – Toss to Right Hand

Horizontal Twirl – Toss to Right Hand

1. In this variation, execute the horizontal twirl with your left hand, tossing upward just high enough to maintain the horizontal movement and cross to your right hand. Catch the baton and continue the horizontal twirl.

Wrist Twirl – Right Hand

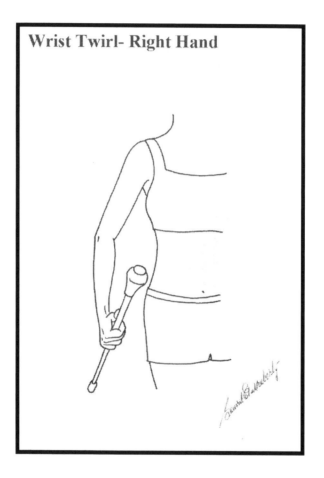

Wrist Twirl – Right Hand

1. Your arm will be straight down at your side. Hold the baton at the middle of the shaft with your thumb pointed toward the ball.

2. Turn the baton to move the ball forward and down in a circular, vertical motion. Keep your wrist loose.

3. The ball of the baton should pass inside your arm, with the tip passing to the outside. Maintain an erect posture while executing this twirl. Keep your head high and your back straight. Position the left hand on the waist, with the thumb at the back and the fingers together.

Wrist Twirl – Left Hand

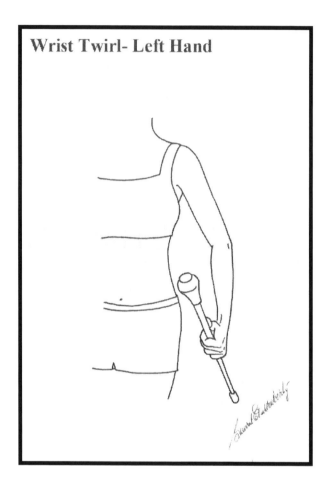

Wrist Twirl – Left Hand

1. Follow the identical instructions for the Right Hand Wrist Twirl, but hold the baton with the left hand, thumb toward the ball.

Remember that the ball of the baton will go inside your arm, and the tip on the outside.

When you practice both the Right and Left Hand Wrist twirls, keep your feet together and hold your head high with your back straight. Keep the unoccupied hand on the waist, with the thumb to the back and the fingers held together.

Forward Inside Circle

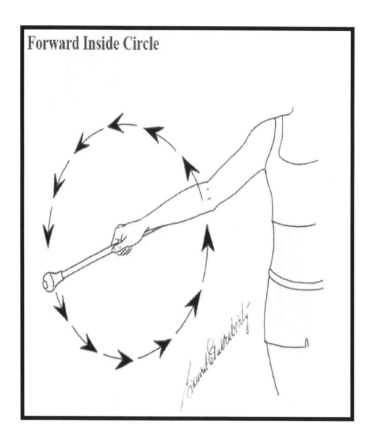

Forward Inside Circle

1. Hold the baton toward the side of the body, keeping the shaft between the thumb and forefinger.

2. To begin this motion, drop the ball away from the body in a downward motion that creates a single circle.

Make sure that the ball passes inside the elbow and the tip to the outside.

As this motion is used frequently with the advanced twirls, practice it in sets of 10 until you've mastered the action.

Backward Inside Circle

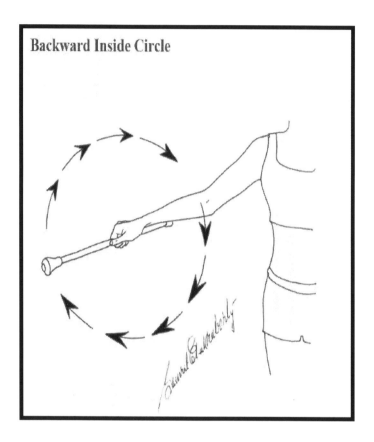

Backward Inside Circle

1. Grasp the baton in the middle of the shaft in the usual fashion with your thumb toward the ball. Move the ball toward the body in a reverse circular motion. Pass the ball to the inside of the elbow and the tip to the outside.

Like all circle motions, this twirl is used extensively for advanced movements, so be sure you can perform it smoothly and uniformly before moving on.

Forward Outside Circle

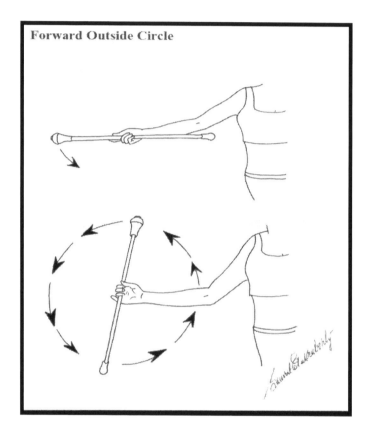

Forward Outside Circle

Forward Outside Circle

1. Hold the baton to the side of the body with the thumb toward the ball.

2. Begin the twirl by moving the ball of the baton away from the body in a downward motion that creates a vertical circle.

Always pass the ball outside the elbow and the tip to the inside.

Like the Forward Inside Circle, this is a motion used extensively in advanced twirls, so practice the movement until you can do it consistently and well.

Backward Outside Circle

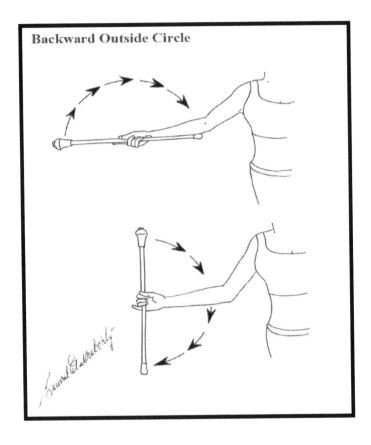

Backward Outside Circle

1. Hold the baton in the usual fashion to then side of your body.

2. Begin the movement by bringing the ball toward the shoulder, allowing it to fall to the outside of the elbow in reverse fashion. Make a complete circle.

The ball of the baton should always pass on the outside of the elbow and the tip to the inside.

Repeat this motion until you can perform it smoothly and consistently. It is used extensively in advanced twirls.

Front Two Hand Spin

Front Two Hand Spin

Front Two Hand Spin

1. Hold the baton in your right hand, this time with your thumb toward the tip, and the ball of the baton to your right.

2. Turn the baton over so that the bottom of your wrist is pointed up.

3. Lay your left hand on top of the baton with the palm up.

4. Hook the thumb of your left hand under the shaft.

5. Allow the baton to go into the left hand.

6. Turn the baton over so that the knuckles of your left hand are up.

7. Put the right hand beside your left hand, knuckles up.

8. Take your left hand off the baton.

9. Start the sequence over.

Front Two Hand Spin - Pass Around Waist

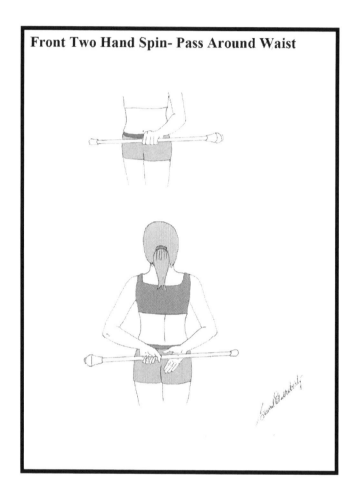

Front Two Hand Spin- Pass Around Waist

Front Two Hand Spin - Pass Around Waist

1. Start with the two hand spin.

2. When the baton is in your left hand, bring it round your waist and into your right hand.

3. At this time you can add another fundamental twirl or trick, or continue the regular Front Two Hand Spin.

A natural continuation of the Front Two Hand Spin is Pass Around the Waist. These two movements are often combined to create a smooth transition from one twirl to the next without a break.

Front Two Hand Spin – Pass Around Knees

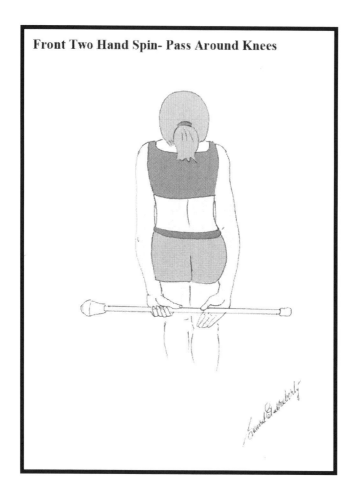

Front Two Hand Spin- Pass Around Knees

Front Two Hand Spin - Pass Around the Knees

1. Begin this sequence with a Front Two Hand Spin.

2. When the baton is in the left hand, pass it around the knees and into your right hand.

Be sure to keep your feet and knees together and closed. Look straight ahead toward your audience, not down toward the ground or floor.

Front Wheel – Right Hand

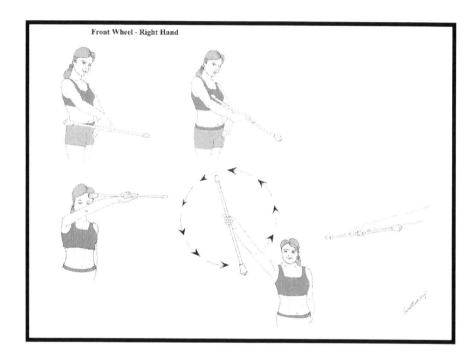

Front Wheel - Right Hand

1. Place the baton in your right hand with your thumb toward the tip. Keep your hand directly over your left foot and maintain a straight alignment with your elbow.

2. Do a single backward wrist twirl with the tip of the baton moving toward your waist.

3. Stop.

4. With the baton still at waist level and leading with the tip, "draw" the shape of a half moon moving toward the right.

5. Keep your arm straight, holding your elbow locked as if you were holding a torch like the Statue of Liberty.

6. Do a single forward outside circle and bring the tip straight down and back to your original starting point.

7. Begin again and repeat multiple times.

Your goal is to speed up and smooth out the motion until it looks like a rolling wheel. Always keep your back straight, head high, and feet together.

Keep the hand you are not using on your hip, holding the fingers together.

Chapter 3 – Advanced Twirling Moves

Four Finger Twirl

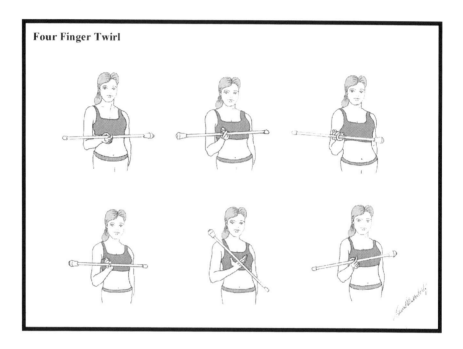

Four Finger Twirl

1. Hold the baton in your left hand between your first and second fingers.

2. Turn the baton to the second finger and allow it to roll to the third and then into the little finger.

3. Roll the baton out of the linger finger and across the backs of the fingers near your knuckles and into the the palm.

4. This returns the baton to its starting position for this twirl and you are ready to begin again.

Horizontal Split Finger Twirl

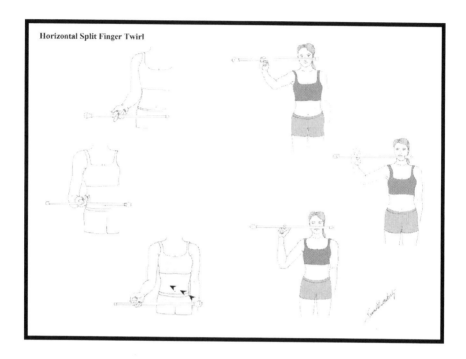

Horizontal Split Finger Twirl

1. Hold the baton with your left hand, ball pointed toward the left, with the shaft sitting between your first and second fingers.

2. Rotate the baton on the horizontal to the second finger, and then to the third.

Since you will not take the baton past the third finger for this twirl, you may want to tape the third and fourth fingers together to ensure the correct hand placement.

3. Bring the ball of the baton under your arm in a horizontal twirl, which you will continue while raising your hand.

4. Turn the baton to the middle finger, and then the index finger.

5. Lower the baton while it is still in the first finger position to begin this twirl again.

Front Wheel – Left Hand

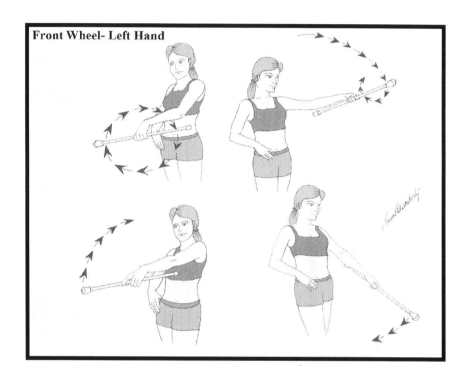

Front Wheel- Left Hand

Front Wheel - Left Hand

1. With the baton in your left hand, thumb toward the ball, position the baton directly over your right food. Keep your elbow straight.

2. Execute one backward wrist twirl. Bring the ball of the baton toward your waist and stop.

3. Beginning at the level of your waist on the right side and leading with the ball of the baton, draw the shape of a half moon over and toward the left.

4. Execute one forward outside circle, with the ball of the baton on the outside of the elbow in the twirl and the tip coming toward the inside.

5. Return to your starting position by bringing the baton straight down.

Time Toss

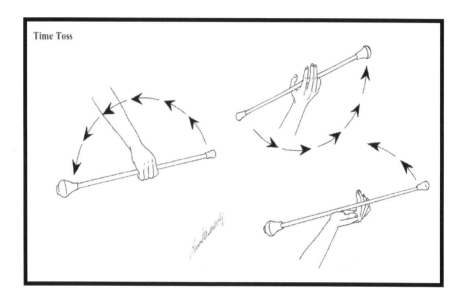

Time Toss

Time Toss

1. With the baton in your right hand and held at your waist, keep your thumb pointing toward the tip and your buckles up.

2. Quickly turn your hand over with the tip going to the right. Your palm will be open.

3. Push off the thumb in an upward motion.

4. Your baton should complete a circle or revolution and you will catch the baton with your thumb toward the tip with the same hand.

The first few times that you try this twirl, you will find it hard to get the baton to move in a full circle and catch it. Be prepared for a lot of drops!

As soon you master one revolution, keep building on your success until you can perform 15-20 repetitions successfully.

Keep your feet together, head high, shoulders back. Your left hand should be at your waist, fingers together, and thumb back.

Twirl Around The Body

Twirl Around The Body

Twirl Around the Body

1. Place your baton in your right hand, thumb toward the ball, left hand on hip.

2. Do one Figure 8 to the side.

3. At waist height, take the ball of the baton and dip it behind the body. Your left hand will reach behind you to take hold of the center of the shaft, with your thumb toward the tip. Your palms are turned outward, facing away from your body.

4. Release the shaft with your right hand and place your hand on your right hip.

5. Extend the baton straight out from your left side and perform a backward outside circle, keeping the tip of the baton on the outside of your arm.

6. With the tip of the baton leading, bring the baton in front of the body in a high horizontal position over the head. Grasp the baton with your right hand, thumb toward the ball, removing your left hand.

7. Bring the top down into a vertical position with a straight motion. The ball should be on top, with the tip at the bottom on the right side.

8. Begin the sequence again to repeat the twirl.

Twirl Around Body – Under Legs

Twirl Around The Body- Under Legs

Twirl Around the Body - Under the Legs

1. With the baton in your right hand and the thumb toward the ball, perform a Figure Eight to the side of the body.

2. Bring your right leg up to the level of your waist with the toe pointed down.

3. Lead with the ball of the baton as you bring it under your raised leg.

---

4. Take hold of the baton with your opposite hand, thumb to tip.

5. Extend the baton in a straight line out to your left side and perform a single backwards circle with the ip moving on the outside of your arm.

6. Lead with the tip of the baton as you bring it to a high horizontal position in front of your body and over your head. Your right hand will grasp the shaft, with the thumb toward the ball.

7. Take away your left hand.

8. Bring the baton into a vertical position pointing straight down with the ball at the top.

9. Bring your left leg to waist level with the toe pointed down.

10. Perform a single Figure Eight leading with the ball of the baton as you bring the baton under your leg, repeating the same sequence of moves as described above.

Cartwheel

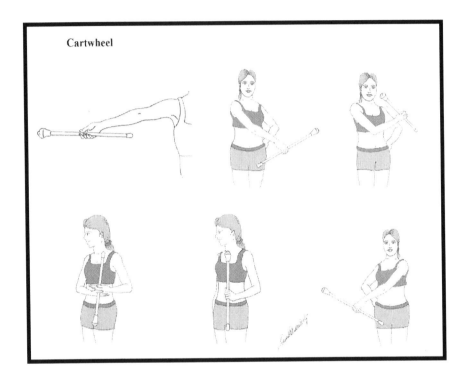

Cartwheel

1. Take the baton in your right hand with your thumb facing toward the ball.

2. Dip across the body to the left side leading with the ball of the baton as in a Figure 8.

3. Don't complete the Figure 8. Leave the baton at your side. Turn the tip up, with the palm of your hand facing up as well.

4. Put your left hand over the right palm, hands touching, and put the baton in the crook of your left thumb.

5. Remove your right hand.

6. With your left thumb take a firm hold on the baton, and turn the left hand over so the ball of the baton is up.

7. Dip the baton to the right side across your body.

8. With the baton on your right side, turn the tip up so that your palm is facing skyward. Put your right hand over your left palm so your hands are touching. Put the baton in the crook of your right thumb.

9. Remove your left hand.

10. Your right thumb should take a firm hold on the baton. Turn your hand over so the ball of the baton is up.

11. Dip the baton across your body to the left side.

12. Repeat.

Cartwheels – Catch Behind Back

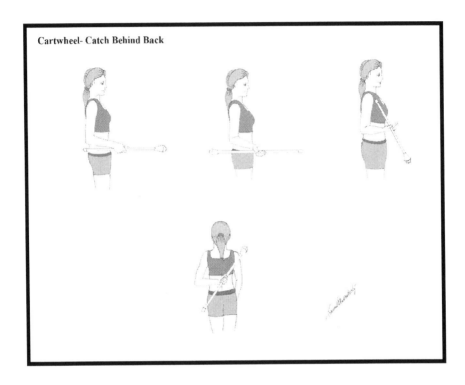

Cartwheel- Catch Behind Back

Cartwheel - Catch Behind the Back

1. Take the baton in your right hand, pointing your thumb toward the ball.

2. Position your left hand behind your back. Keep the palm open and pointed upward.

3. Execute a cartwheel in your right hand at your side followed by a small push upward.

4. Catch with your left hand behind your back and bring the baton out on your left side.

5. Put your right hand behind your be hick with the palm open and pointed upward.

6. Execute a cartwheel with your left hand at your side followed by a small push upward.

7. Catch with your right hand behind your back and bring the baton out on your right side.

8. Repeat.

Cartwheels – Under Legs

Cartwheels - Under Legs

1. Hold the baton in your right hand with your thumb pointing toward the ball.

2. Bring your right leg up, pointing your toe down.

3. Put your left hand under your leg moving from the inside.

4. Execute a cartwheel with your right hand and take the baton into your left hand coming from under your leg to the left side.

5. Put your right hand under your left leg and execute a cartwheel with your left hand.

6. Take the baton in your right hand coming from under your leg to the right side.

7. Repeat.

Reverse

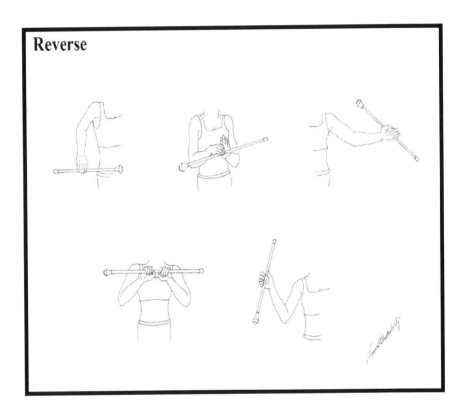

Reverse

1. Holding the baton in your right hand with the thumb toward the ball, draw a circle, passing the ball under your arm.

2. Execute a Front Two Hand Spin.

3. Take the baton in your left hand and do a backwards outside circle.

4. Pass the baton in front and take it in your right hand to perform a forward outside circle on the right side.

5. Begin a repeat of this twirl by drawing a circle under the right arm.

Double Reverse

Double Reverse

1. With the baton in your right hand, thumb toward the ball (left hand on hip), perform a Figure 8 at the side.

2. At the level of your waist, dip the ball behind the back while reaching behind with your left hand, which will grasp the baton at the center of the shaft, thumb toward the tip. Your palms will be turned out and away from your body.

3. Release the baton with your right hand, moving your hand to your hip.

4. With the left hand, move the baton out to the side where you will execute a backwards outside circle. (Be sure to circle outside of your arm.)

5. With the tip of the baton in the lead, pass behind the back with your palms turned out. Take the baton in your right hand behind your back with the thumb toward the ball.

6. Release with your left hand and put your hand on your hip.

7. Move the baton out from behind your back and to the right where you will begin the twirl again with a Figure 8 at your side.

Chapter 4 – Tricks and Fancy Moves

Lariat Rope

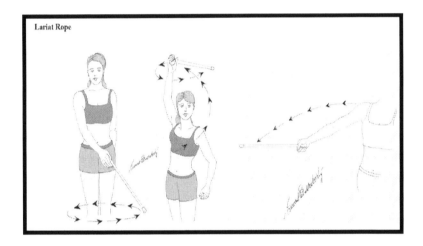

Lariat Rope

1. Grasp the ball of the baton loosely, pointing downward. Draw a horizontal circle from left to right.

2. Next, circle over your head once from the left to the right shoulder keeping the motion of the twirl flat, like a plate.

3. When you reach the right shoulder, bring the baton back in front of your body.

4. Lift your left leg straight out in front with the toe pointed and move the baton under the raised leg.

5. Quickly put your left leg down and raise the right leg out straight with toe pointed down and continue moving the baton under the right leg.

Lariat Rope Around Ankle

Lariat Rope Around Ankle

1. Grasp the ball of the baton loosely, pointing downward. Draw a horizontal circle from left to right.

2. Next, circle over your head once from the left to the right shoulder keeping the motion of the twirl flat, like a plate.

3. When you reach the right shoulder, bring the baton back in front of your body.

4. Lift your left leg straight out in front with the toe pointed and move the baton under the raised leg.

5. Quickly put your left leg down and raise the right knee to the level of your waist, toe pointed down.

6. Allow the baton to roll horizontally across the front of your right ankle and catch it in your left hand.

Body Roll

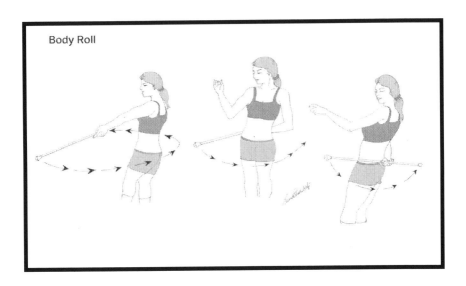

Body Roll

1. Hold the baton at the tip in your left hand and take a wide complete swing from left to right around your body.

2. As the baton comes to your right side, allow the shaft to hit your body at a position about two-thirds of the way down from the ball.

3. Make the catch with your right hand in back of your body.

The catch will be easier to make if you raise your left hand straight up and out of the way, or make sure the right hand is on the outside of the left hand for the catch.

Palm Spin

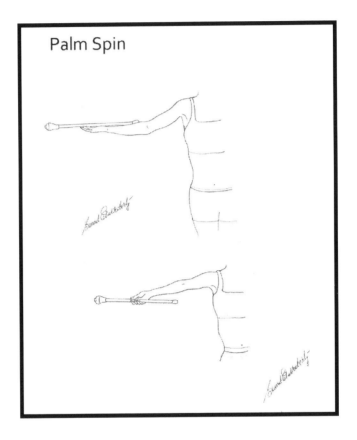

Palm Spin

1. Perform a Horizontal Twirl with the ball on top, tip on bottom.

2. Open the hand flat, keeping your fingers together.

3. Let the baton spin slowly on the palm.

4. Take the baton back into the Horizontal Twirl.

When you practice this move, keep your head high with a straight alignment to your back and your feet together. Keep the hand that is not in use on your waist or hip with the fingers together.

Palm Spin Over Head

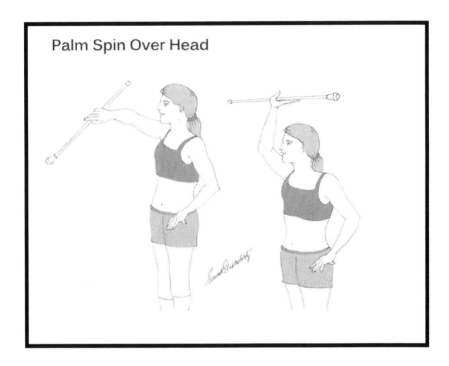

Palm Spin Over Head

1. Do a series of horizontal twirls with your right hand and stop.

2. Leading with your wrist, bring the baton directly over your head allowing the knuckles to touch your hair.

3. Open the palm of your hand flat and let the baton spin on the flattened surface.

4. Take the baton back into a horizontal twirl while lowering it to the extreme right of your body.

5. Repeat.

You will want to keep your palm close to the top of your head so if the baton falls, it will fall away from you.

Fingertip Twirl

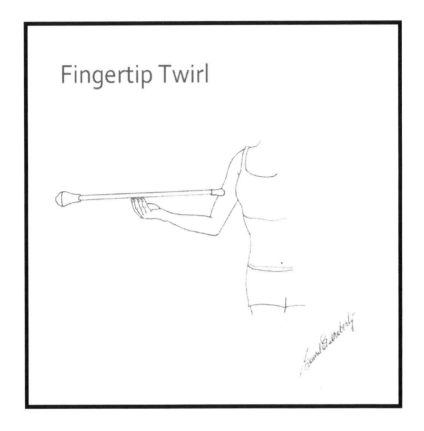

Fingertip Twirl

1. Perform a horizontal twirl, then stop and make a table with your fingers.

2. Using your thumb to move the baton, make sure it stays on top of your four fingers.

3. Make the motion of the baton perfectly flat, keeping it on the horizontal.

4. Take the baton into our hand and complete another Horizontal Twirl.

Corkscrew (Grapevine)

Corkscrew (Grapevine)

1. Take hold of the baton with your right hand, grasping it by the ball. Circle the baton over your head and bring it around and behind your neck, grasping it with your left hand.

2. Push your left hand down toward the tip of the baton, then take the baton by the tip and bring it around the back. Make sure that your right arm is on the outside in a position to make the catch.

3. Roll the baton across the waist and catch with the right hand on the left side.

4. Take the baton in your right hand and bring it across the front to the back of the knees, taking it with your left hand on the right side.

5. Slide your hand to the tip of the baton and bring it across the front to the back of the ankle.

6. Roll the baton across the front of the ankles and catch with the right hand.

Leg Roll 1

Leg Roll 1

1. With your right hand, hold the tip of the baton.

2. Raise your right leg up to a level position with the toe pointed downward.

3. Bring the baton under the right leg.

4. As you release the baton to roll it across the top of the right leg, press the knuckles of the right hand into the outside of the right leg. Open your hand to receive the baton.

Leg Roll 2

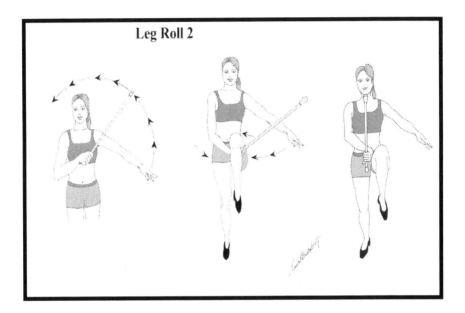

Leg Roll 2

1. Hold the baton by the ball with your right hand.

2. Make one large circle in the front.

3. Bring your left leg up to a level position with the toe pointed down.

4. Pass the baton under the left leg.

5. As you release the baton to roll it across the top of your legs, press the knuckles of your hand into the inside or your leg. Open your hand to receive the baton.

Leg Roll 3

Leg Roll 3

1. With your right hand, hold the baton by the tip.

2. Make a large circle in front of your body.

3. Bring your left leg up to a level position with your toe pointed down.

4. Pass the baton under your left leg.

5. As the baton rolls across the top of your left from the left to the right, your left hand will reach under your leg to catch the baton.

Leg Roll 3 with Ankle Roll

Leg Roll 3 with Ankle Roll

Leg Roll 3 with Ankle Roll

1. Follow the instructions for the Leg Roll 3.

2. Take the baton by the ball with your thumb pointing toward the tip.

3. Bring your foot and leg to the left until the foot is back and level with the knee.

4. Roll the baton over your left ankle and catch it with your left hand on top of the back side of the ankle.

Elbow Roll

Elbow Roll

1. Take the baton in your right hand about the three quarters of the way down the shaft with your thumb pointing toward the ball.

2. Put your left fist in the middle of your chest with the elbow bent and the arm held horizontally in a position level with the shoulder.

3. Bring the baton under your bend elbow and let it roll across the top of the elbow. Give a little push up with the elbow as the baton rolls across.

4. Catch the baton on the right side while it is still in the vertical position with your thumb pointed toward the ball.

Double Elbow Roll

Double Elbow Roll

1. With your right hand, hold the baton about three quarters of the way down the shaft with the thumb pointed toward the ball.

2. Place your left fist in the middle of your chest at the level of your shoulder on the horizontal with the elbow bent.

3. Pass the baton under your bent elbow and let it roll across the top, giving a slight upward push with the elbow as the baton rolls across.

4. When you release the baton to roll over the elbow, immediately bring the right elbow up and over the right end of the baton, pushing down with the right elbow. The baton will roll over the right elbow.

5. Quickly reach down under the right elbow with your left hand and catch the baton with your thumb toward the ball.

Horizontal Leg Bounce

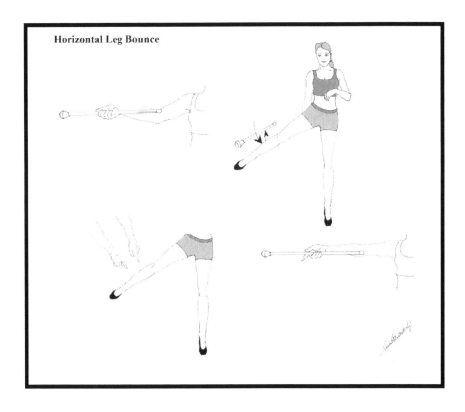

Horizontal Leg Bounce

Horizontal Leg Bounce

1. Hold the baton in your right hand with your thumb toward the ball.

2. Start a horizontal twirl. When the baton is in motion, make a slight upward toss to the right and bounce the baton off the extended portion of your right leg in the "strike zone."

3. Catch the baton in the horizontal position, keeping your thumb toward the ball.

Chapter 5 - Jumps and Leaps

Straddle Jump 1

Straddle Jump 1

1. Stand with your feet together and do two Front Hand Spins.

2. Stop.

3. With your feet about two feet apart, jump. Lock your knees and bend forward at the waist.

4. Bring the ball of the baton between your legs until the tip is past the legs and then bring the ball out.

5. As the ball is moved out, jump and bring the feet back together.

6. Finish the movement with two Front Hand Spins.

Make sure that the bend from the waist is perfectly straight and always lock your knees to preserve the line. Keep your feet pointing straight ahead.

Straddle Jump 2

Straddle Jump 2

1. With the ball of the baton in your right hand and the tip in your left, hold the baton directly overhead with your arms straight and your elbows locked.

2. With your feet about two feet apart and knees locked, jump and bend forward from the waist.

3. Bring the baton under your legs until the tip has past through, then turn the baton around and bring the ball out.

4. As the ball moves forward, jump, bringing your feet together. Return the baton to the overhead position where you began to end the twirl.

Split Jump

Split Jump

Split Jump

The Split Jump is basic and straightforward. The right leg should be fairly straight, extended forward, and the left leg should be equally straight extended backwards.

Just before leaving the ground, bend your knees slightly. Spring from the ball of the foot and land there as well. Practice executing these motions smoothly, and keeping your legs as straight as possible.

Spread Eagle Jump

Spread Eagle Jump

The Spread Eagle is another basic jump. As with the Split Jump, bend your knees slightly as you are leaving the ground, springing up from the fall of the foot and landing there as well.

The goal in this jump is to bring your legs to the side as far as possible, keeping the legs in straight alignment. The best way to get good at any jump is practice, practice, practice.

Chapter 6 - Aerials

Flash Leg – Pull Out

Flash Leg- Pull Out

Flash Leg - Pull Out

1. Take hold of the baton at the tip with your right hand, thumb pointed toward the ball.

2. Raise your right leg level with your waist, toe pointed downward and pass the baton under your knee.

3. With the baton pressed against your right leg, bring the leg to extreme right.

4. Pull the baton out when you get to the right side and end with your feet together.

Simple Flash

Simple Flash

1. With your right hand, hold the baton by the ball.

2. With a forward motion, circle at the left side, then use the same circular motion on the right.

3. Circle under your left leg with a forward motion and bring the baton around the right ankle.

4. Take the baton in your left hand to end the twirl.

Chapter 7 – Flash Series

High Aerial in Front by Tip

High Aerial in Front By Tip

High Aerial in Front By Tip

1. With your right hand, hold the baton by the tip.

2. Make a complete circle in front of your body. When the ball passes your right foot, give it a small upward push.

3. Keep your eyes on the center of the baton's shaft as it comes down.

4. At a level slightly above your head, reach out with your right hand. Your palm should be out and your knuckles toward your body. Grab the baton at the center of the shaft.

As you begin to work on aerials, start out with very gentle throws so you can keep your eyes on the center of the baton's shaft. It is extremely important that you don't take your eyes off the baton until you have caught it again. As you develop accuracy, you can work on harder and higher throws.

Time Toss – Catch Behind Back

Time Toss- Catch Behind Back

Time Toss - Catch Behind Back

1. Hold the baton at the level of your waist in your right hand. Your thumb should point toward the tip, and your knuckles should be up.

2. Start a Time Toss, pushing the baton up a little above the head.

3. Keep your eyes on the baton and turn quickly to the right moving your right hand behind your back at the same time to watch the Time Toss as it comes down.

Horizontal – Catch Behind Back

Horizontal - Catch Behind Back

1. Hold the baton with your left hand, thumb toward the ball. Perform left horizontal twirls. While the baton is spinning, push it up and over your head.

2. Put your right hand behind your back quickly and turn to the right looking over your left shoulder to keep your eyes on the baton.

3. Bend your head down and catch the baton behind your back with your right hand.

Time Toss – High in Front

Time Toss - High in Front

1. Perform a Time Toss, raising your right hand just as the baton rolls off your thumb.

2. As the baton comes down, keep your eyes on the center of the staff. When the baton is just above your head, reach with your right hand, keeping the palm out and your knuckles toward your body.

3. Grasp the baton in the center of the shaft.

Chapter 8 – Marching Routines

Marching Routines - Parade Marching

At the pre-arranged signal from the drum major's whistle, bring your baton into the horizontal position shown in the first illustration.

Count 1-2-3-4 while marching and then move the baton over to the other side for another count of 4.

Repeat the above on the left side for a count of 4, then the right side for a count of 4.

Bring the baton up on the left side and do a step / close step. Move to the right side and repeat.

Repeat on each side.

Your baton will then go on your arm for four marching steps.

Stretch your arms out. The arm with the baton goes out front first. March four steps.

Stretch your arms out again. The arm with the baton goes in back. March four steps.

Hold the baton near the ball and swing it across the front of the waist to the left. The left arm goes straight up with the hand flat. March four steps.

Raise your right arms with the baton on it and place your left hand on your waist. March four steps.

Bring the baton down to the regular position on the arm and finish the routine by marching with the baton on arm.

Marching Routine 2

While marching, do a horizontal twirl in front for four counts followed by a horizontal in back for four counts.

Bring the baton under your elbows as shown in the illustration and march four steps.

Take a step up and step kick, returning the baton to rest on the arms while marching.

Chapter 9 - Relevant Websites

The World of Batontwirling.com
www.batontwirling.com

World Baton Twirling Federation
www.wbtf.org

National Baton Twirling Association Europe - NBTA - EUROPE
www.nbta-europe.info/en/

United States Twirling Association - Baton Twirling
www.ustwirling.com

Twirl Mania
www.twirlmania.com

American Baton Company-Baton Twirling Supplies
www.americanbaton.com

World Twirling Batons
www.worldtwirling.com

National Coalition for the Advancement of Baton Twirling
www.ncabt.com

Baton Twirling, etc.
www.batontwirlingetc.com

Texas Twirlers Baton Twirling
www.texastwirlers.com

Twirl Planet Twirling Batons and Majorette Supplies
www.twirlplanet.com

Star Line Baton
www.starlinebaton.com

How would you like FREE access to some great Baton Twirling videos?

We've discovered some great videos around the web showing all the baton twirling moves you'll need!

Simply go to

http://www.BatonTwirlingMaster.com

and join for FREE!

You'll receive the videos showing the basic moves and some fun tricks. All delivered to your inbox.

Contact Me

If you have any questions / suggestions about this book please get in contact. You can email me directly at Susan@Bleppublishing.com

We all love Baton Twirling - Let's go and enjoy our passion.